FIRST-PERSON STORIES OF THE

MOON LANDING

BY KATE MIKOLEY

AF904430

ROSEN PUBLISHING PRIMARY SOURCE LIBRARY

ROSEN PUBLISHING

Published in 2027 by The Rosen Publishing Group, Inc.
2544 Clinton Street, Buffalo, NY 14224

Copyright © 2027 by The Rosen Publishing Group, Inc.

All rights reserved. No part of this book may be reproduced in any form without permission in writing from the publisher, except by a reviewer.

Designer: Deanna Lepovich
Editor: Nicole Horning

Cataloging-in-Publication Data

Names: Mikoley, Kate.
Title: First-person stories of the moon landing / Kate Mikoley.
Description: Buffalo, NY : Rosen Publishing, 2027. | Series: The Rosen Publishing primary source library | Includes glossary and index.
Identifiers: ISBN 9781725343078 (pbk.) | ISBN 9781725343085 (library bound) | ISBN 9781725343092 (ebook)
Subjects: LCSH: Project Apollo (U.S.)–History–Juvenile literature. | Space flight to the moon–History–Juvenile literature.
Classification: LCC TL789.8.U6 M55 2027 | DDC 629.454–dc23

Some of the images in this book illustrate individuals who are models. The depictions do not imply actual situations or events.

Manufactured in the United States of America

CPSIA Compliance Information: Batch #CSRYA27. For further information, contact Rosen Publishing at 1-800-237-9932.

Find us on

CONTENTS

FOREWORD

History is so much more than just a boring collection of names and dates. It is a collection of stories—sometimes tragic stories, sometimes heroic stories, sometimes romantic stories, sometimes scary stories. And they're all stories of real people who lived real lives.

Those stories can get lost in the shuffle of memorizing battles, studying maps, and listing important court cases or rulers. That's why primary sources are so valuable. They remind us that historical events happened to and because of real people. Reading diaries, looking at photographs, and seeing newspaper articles are just some ways to make history feel personal through primary sources.

Another way is through watching or listening to interviews with people who lived through major historical events. That's what you're invited to do in this book—and all the books that are part of *The Rosen Publishing Primary Source Library*. Each chapter includes quotes from an interview with a real person who experienced a major historical event in a deeply personal way. You can also scan the QR code included at the beginning of each chapter to watch a video interview with the person featured in that chapter.

Created in partnership with Generations Broadcasting, *The Rosen Publishing Primary Source Library* was created to remind readers that there is power in sharing our stories. First-person stories make history come alive. And when history comes alive, we're better able to learn from it—and avoid the mistakes of the past.

The events you're living through today will be part of the next generation's history lessons. As you read and watch the stories collected here, think about what you want your story to be.

Note: More interviews about the topics featured in this series, as well as many other historical events, can be accessed via a subscription to Rosen Publishing's GBC Stories Database: rosendigital.com/GBCStories/.

HOW TO WATCH THE INTERVIEWS FEATURED IN THIS BOOK

- Use your phone's camera, and hold it over the QR code.
- Click the link that appears.
- Watch the video that pops up. If you would like to read a transcript of the interview while you watch, you can click on that option next to the video screen.

INTRODUCTION

Apollo 11 was the lunar mission that brought American astronauts Neil Armstrong and Edwin (Buzz) Aldrin Jr. to the moon, where they became the first people to walk on its surface. The historic moon landing happened on July 20, 1969, but the effort to get there started years earlier.

Eight years before *Apollo 11* launched, the Soviet Union sent the first human into space on April 12, 1961. Soon after this flight, in which **cosmonaut** Yuri Gagarin made one orbit around Earth reaching a maximum altitude of 187 miles (301 km), President John F. Kennedy made it known that he intended for the United States to win the **Space Race**. Less than a month later, Alan Shepard became the first American in space, though he did not orbit Earth. Then, on May 25, 1961, Kennedy announced his goal for the country to land a man on the moon and then get him back to Earth safely before the end of the decade. The effort of the National **Aeronautics** and Space Administration (NASA) to get people safely to the moon and back, called the Apollo Program, began to really take off following the president's remark.

After significant study and feats of engineering, uncrewed Apollo test missions began in 1966 using a vehicle known as the Saturn V rocket to launch the spacecraft on its course toward the moon. In 1967, a fire broke out on the *Apollo 1* spacecraft during a ground rehearsal. Sadly, three astronauts—Virgil Grissom, Edward White, and Roger Chaffee—were killed. This delayed the first crewed Apollo flight and resulted in NASA making changes to improve mission safety.

In October 1968, *Apollo 7* orbited Earth, carrying three astronauts and completing the Apollo program's first manned space mission. Three more missions happened before *Apollo 11* launched in 1969 carrying Commander Neil Armstrong, Lunar Module Pilot Buzz Aldrin, and Command Module Pilot Michael Collins.

On July 16, the three astronauts onboard *Apollo 11* launched from Cape Kennedy—now known as Cape Canaveral—in Florida. The country was captivated by the mission. About 1 million people, including Vice President Spiro Agnew and former President Lyndon

In all, the *Eagle* spent 21 hours and 38 minutes on the moon's surface. In this photo of Aldrin, you can see Armstrong's reflection on the visor of Aldrin's helmet.

B. Johnson, watched the liftoff from the ground at Cape Kennedy. Millions more watched from home. Over the next several days, people continued to follow the journey by watching news coverage and **transmissions** from the spacecraft on television.

Then, on July 20, Aldrin and Armstrong crawled through a tunnel from the Command Module *Columbia* into the Lunar Module *Eagle*. Collins stayed behind to pilot *Columbia*, as *Eagle* split off toward the moon. At 4:17 p.m. U.S. Eastern Daylight Time (EDT), Armstrong radioed mission control to let them know the *Eagle* had landed on the moon. Hours later, at 10:56 p.m., Armstrong emerged from the craft and became the first person to set foot on the moon.

About 20 minutes later, Aldrin joined Armstrong. The pair walked on the surface of the moon for more than two hours. They set up devices that would continue to be used to study the moon's environment after they left, collected rock and soil samples, and took many photographs documenting the journey.

CHAPTER ONE

PREVIOUS PIONEERS

Before you can get to the moon, you have to get to space. That was the goal of the United States's Project Mercury. More specifically, the program aimed to get an American into orbit around Earth and bring him back safely and alive. John Glenn would later turn out to be the first American to do that.

But first, the U.S. space program needed to understand the technical requirements and medical effects of sending a human into space. And time was of the essence. The United States and Soviet Union were in the middle of the Cold War. Each nation was trying to prove their superiority and influence to the rest of the world, so getting to space first was a huge motivator in the rivalry. But when the Soviet Union reached that milestone first, the United States was not ready to give up the race. If anything, it just gave the space program more reason to succeed.

A NEW PROGRAM

In 1958, President Dwight D. Eisenhower signed the National Aeronautics and Space Act, creating NASA. A few months later, NASA's first human spaceflight program, Project Mercury, began.

Scan this QR code to watch a video about John Glenn and his historic journey to become the first American to orbit Earth.

One of the first things needed to get a person into space was a suit that would keep them safe. John Glenn is seen here in his Mercury suit, designed to keep the astronaut safe in the event of depressurization in the cabin.

NASA's first seven astronauts were chosen to be part of Project Mercury in 1959. They would become known as the Mercury 7.

To become part of the Mercury 7, one had to have been a military test pilot. They were required to have graduated from test pilot school and have more than 1,500 hours of jet flight time. They also had to be under 40 years old, shorter than 5 feet 11 inches

Launched by the Soviet Union in 1957, Sputnik 1 was the first artificial Earth satellite, and one of the main triggers to the start of the Space Race. A replica of the satellite is shown here.

FAST FACT

BEFORE NASA, THE NATIONAL ADVISORY COMMITTEE FOR AERONAUTICS (NACA) WAS THE FEDERAL AGENCY THAT HEADED AERONAUTICAL RESEARCH IN THE UNITED STATES. NACA WAS FOUNDED IN 1915 AND WAS ABSORBED INTO NASA AFTER IT WAS ESTABLISHED.

(1.8 m) tall, in excellent physical condition, and have obtained a bachelor's degree or equivalent. More than 500 graduates from U.S. Navy and Air Force pilot schools were screened. From that group, 110 were considered qualified. From there, candidates were further evaluated and narrowed down, with many going through classified briefings, medical examinations, and rigorous testing. Eventually, the seven men were chosen. They were Alan Shepard, Gus Grissom, John Glenn, Scott Carpenter, Walter Schirra, Gordon Cooper, and Deke Slayton.

THE MERCURY 7

While NASA has always been a **civilian** organization, President Eisenhower thought the Mercury Program astronauts should be military test pilots. The men who were selected became American heroes quickly.

Alan Shepard was the first of the seven—and the first American—to go to space. On May 5, 1961, he made a 15-minute **suborbital** flight in *Freedom 7*. Years later, he became the fifth man to walk on the moon.

Just two months after Shepard's first flight, Virgil "Gus" Grissom made a similar trip on the *Liberty 7*. He flew in space once more and was chosen to command the first manned Apollo mission. Sadly, he was one of the people killed in a fire during the January 27, 1967, preflight test for *Apollo 1*.

John Glenn was the third of the Mercury 7 to go to space. He did so on February 20, 1962, becoming the first American to orbit Earth. Three months later, Scott Carpenter completed a similar mission onboard *Aurora 7*.

Walter Schirra flew on *Sigma 7* in 1962. He was the only astronaut to have flown in the Mercury, Gemini, and Apollo missions.

Each member of the Mercury 7 was a former military pilot, having served in the U.S. Navy, Air Force, or Marines.

In May 1963, Gordon Cooper went to space on *Faith 7*. He went to space a second time during the Gemini Program.

Donald "Deke" Slayton was the only Mercury 7 astronaut who did not go to space during the Mercury program. A heart condition prevented him from going for many years, but he did eventually make it to space as part of the **Apollo-Soyuz Test Project**.

FAST FACT

WOMEN WERE NOT ALLOWED TO BE MILITARY PILOTS AT THE TIME, AND BECAUSE OF RACIAL DISCRIMINATION, VERY FEW MILITARY TEST PILOTS WERE MEN OF COLOR. THIS ESSENTIALLY MADE IT SO ONLY WHITE MEN QUALIFIED TO BE PART OF THE MERCURY 7.

GET TO KNOW GLENN

While he wasn't the first person—let alone the first American—to go to space, John Glenn became especially well-known. When the Mercury 7 was asked who wanted to go to space first, all seven men raised their hands. John Glenn famously raised both of his.

The video gives a brief but impressive overview of Glenn's credentials:

> *Astronaut John Glenn of New Concord, Ohio. Lieutenant Colonel, United States Marine Corps. Married, father of two teenage children, Glenn has been a pilot over half of his 40 years, has flown in two wars, and is a veteran test pilot who, five years earlier, established a transcontinental plane record as the first man to average* **supersonic** *speeds across America. He volunteered for space flight, is one of seven astronauts selected for Project Mercury, the man-in-space program directed by the National Aeronautics and Space Administration.*

Glenn's military experience began when he joined the U.S. Naval Reserve in 1942. Then, in 1943, he joined the Marine Corps. He flew 59 missions in World War II and 90 in the Korean War. After he returned from Korea, Glenn attended the U.S. Naval Test Pilot School at Patuxent River, Maryland, where he graduated in 1954. He made the record-breaking flight mentioned in the video in 1957, completing the first transcontinental flight with an average supersonic speed. In this flight, he flew across the country, from California to New York in just 3 hours and 23 minutes.

By the time he was selected to be part of the Mercury 7, Glenn was already an established career pilot, but going to space would literally be stepping into a new frontier. Glenn's orbit of Earth on February 20, 1962, was seen by many as a step toward equalizing the Space Race with the Soviet Union. While Yuri Gagarin was

At 37 years old, John Glenn was the oldest of the Mercury 7 at the time of his selection.

the first to orbit the planet, he had done so only once. Glenn did it three times.

To many, Glenn was seen as a national hero after this flight. In an interview, a woman explained what he meant to her, along with her experience of getting to meet him:

> *He came to our college and spent a whole day...I arranged to meet him, and he was just a charming man—wonderful. He was Colonel Glenn at that time...I was taking classes at that time, and he was lecturing that night too and I left my class to go hear his lecture. But he was back and forth in our office all day long and I will never forget that. He is one of my heroes.*

IN FLIGHT

On the morning of February 20, 1962, Glenn spent nearly four hours in the launch capsule before it took off. A series of delays finally came to an end at 9:47 a.m. EST when the three main engines of the rocket ignited. The rocket launched, bringing Glenn and *Friendship 7* into flight. Five minutes later, Glenn was in orbit!

After the spacecraft was released from the launch vehicle, Glenn could be heard taking in the view:

> *Oh, that view is tremendous. [I] could see the booster during turnaround just a couple of hundred yards behind me. It was beautiful.*

The plan was always for Glenn to make three orbits of the earth, but it would be understandable if you heard the voice of a person from Mercury Control in the video saying, "You have a go, at least seven orbits," and thought that meant they cut the flight short after three. Glenn even responds to this voice by saying, "Roger, understand, go for at least seven orbits."

Although Glenn's mission has been misrepresented in several movies, including *Hidden Figures*, as being intended to have achieved seven orbits, this is not true. The statement was only meant to signify that the spacecraft would be able to go for at least seven orbits, not that it was the plan.

In the end, Glenn circled Earth for the expected three orbits. A few small flukes occurred, including a faulty **thruster** that meant Glenn

Glenn was initially supposed to launch in *Friendship 7* on January 27, 1962, but thick clouds on that day caused the takeoff to be postponed.

John Glenn wanted Katherine Johnson to be the one to check the computer's calculations.

had to control the spacecraft manually. The video explained what occurred:

> *At the end of the first orbit, a thruster malfunction permitted only partial use of the automatic stabilization and control system. Astronaut Glenn took over and controlled the spacecraft manually.*

Despite these challenges, the flight went mostly according to plan. After nearly five hours

FAST FACT

KATHERINE JOHNSON WAS A MATHEMATICIAN WHO CALCULATED SPACECRAFT TRAJECTORIES FOR PROJECT MERCURY. SHE CHECKED THE COMPUTER CALCULATIONS FOR JOHN GLENN'S RETURN TO EARTH BY HAND USING A DESKTOP MECHANICAL CALCULATING MACHINE. HER WORK WAS PORTRAYED IN THE 2016 MOVIE *HIDDEN FIGURES*.

A camera recorded Glenn inside the capsule throughout his three trips around Earth.

FAST FACT

THE NUMBER OF ORBITS WAS SET TO BE THREE BECAUSE AFTER THREE TRIPS AROUND EARTH, IT WAS STILL EASY ENOUGH TO LAND IN THE INTENDED RECOVERY AREA. WITH A FOURTH ORBIT OR MORE, THE ROTATION OF EARTH MAKES IT MORE DIFFICULT FOR THE SPACECRAFT TO LAND WHERE IT IS INTENDED TO GO.

in space, Glenn landed safely in the Atlantic Ocean, and as the video stated, he was "Well within the planned recovery area."

The video also stated that Glenn's voyage had been a success:

> *All mission objectives had been achieved, including a realization of the primary goal of the Mercury Program: to put a man in orbit around the earth and recover him safely.*

The success of this mission was yet another step toward the goal the United States had of landing a man on the moon and safely returning him to Earth.

HOW YOU SEE HISTORY

1. Why was John Glenn's trip to space seen as so important, even though it wasn't the first time someone had gone there?
2. Why do you think age and height were part of the requirements to become part of Mercury 7?
3. What do you think the effect would have been on the future of the U.S. space program had John Glenn's trip in *Friendship 7* not been successful?

CHAPTER TWO

A TEAM EFFORT

Most people know the names of the two people who set foot on the moon on July 20, 1969. But many aren't fully aware of the thousands of other people who helped build the Apollo program and engineer the equipment required to get humans to the moon in the first place. NASA employed scientists, engineers, and **technicians** for the mission. They also contracted with other major companies and universities to develop the equipment and tools needed to safely land people on the moon and return them to Earth.

Bill Ragan's father was one of the many people who helped Americans land on the moon in 1969. Bill also worked on **schematics** and artist conceptions. In an interview, he fondly remembered the part he and his dad played in the historic moment of the moon landing.

WORKING WITH NASA

In 1961, President Kennedy committed to landing a person on the moon. With this announcement, NASA needed to accelerate their plans for building the Apollo spacecraft. North American Aviation (NAA) was selected to be the main

Scan this QR code to watch Bill Ragan speak of his father's involvement in the engineering and design of the Lunar excursion module for *Apollo 11*.

The Lunar Module *Eagle* broke away from the Command Module in lunar orbit to fly to the surface of the moon.

contractor to design and build the spacecraft.

NAA was already a well-known aerospace manufacturer in the United States. It had produced combat aircraft used in World War II; helped develop important navigation, guidance, and data systems; and even had

FAST FACT

NORTH AMERICAN AVIATION NO LONGER EXISTS. THROUGH SEVERAL MERGERS AND SALES, IT BECAME PART OF OTHER COMPANIES. TODAY, WHAT WAS ONCE NAA IS NOW PART OF BOEING.

NAA worked on the earlier Apollo missions too. This photograph shows crews working on an *Apollo 7* spacecraft.

GET TO KNOW THE SPACECRAFT

Imagine spending eight days trapped in a large car with two other people. That's what it was like for the astronauts inside the Apollo Command Module. The module, built specially for the Apollo Program, was just big enough for the three astronauts to live and work during the trip. There were bench-like couches where the astronauts could be strapped in for safety during takeoff and landing, but there was little room for much else. The *Apollo 11* Command Module was known as *Columbia*.

Behind the Command Module was the Service Module. This is where the fuel tanks and engines were kept.

Behind the Service Module was the Lunar Module, known in *Apollo 11* as *Eagle*. A tunnel connected *Eagle* to *Columbia*. Aldrin and Armstrong crawled through the tunnel to get to *Eagle*, which separated

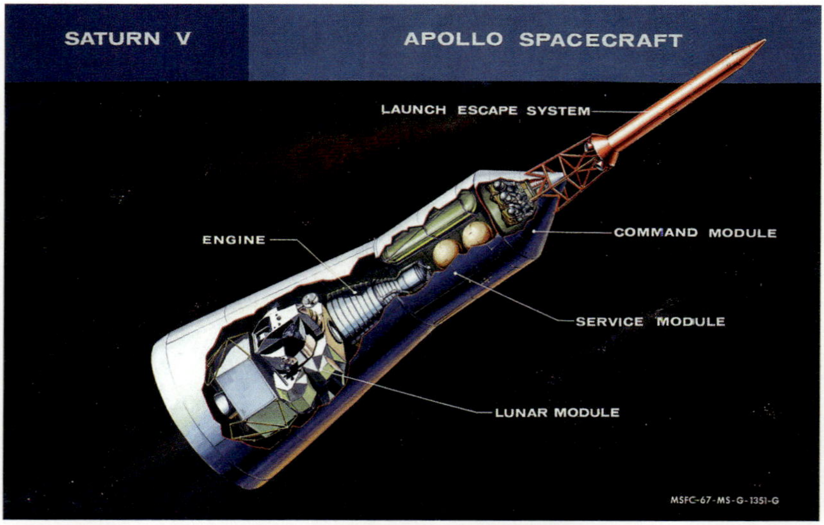

***Columbia* and *Eagle* split apart around the end of the spacecraft's 12th lunar orbit.**

a **nuclear** development division. The company's work with rocket-powered aircraft made them a logical pick as a contractor for the Apollo missions.

Bill Ragan's father was one of many NAA employees who was part of the project. In his interview, Bill explained his father's contributions to the engineering and design in relation to the moon landing:

from *Columbia* before going to the moon. The Command Module stayed in orbit, piloted by Collins, while the Lunar Module took Aldrin and Armstrong to the moon's surface.

Another important part of the spacecraft was the rocket. The Saturn V rocket used for the moon landing mission was more than 360 feet (110 m) tall. It is what lifted the spacecraft from Earth's surface into space, so naturally it had to be strong. It burned over 20 tons (18 tonnes) of fuel at launch and had enough power to carry nearly 4 double-decker buses to the moon! Even today, it is still one of the largest and most powerful rockets ever built.

This photo shows the seats where the three astronauts sat during the flight.

He was not involved with the flights because most of the flights were occurring either out of Houston, Florida, or California... his participation was working in the design field of the Lunar Excursion Module. Certain little parts of it...there were hundreds of engineers working on it. When North American [Aviation] got the contract to work with NASA, he became part of that.

Aldrin is seen here standing next to the leg of the Lunar Module *Eagle*.

A BIG EVENT ON THE SMALL SCREEN

Like others all around the world, Bill Ragan was excited to watch the moon landing on television. He remembers exactly where he was when it happened. In his interview, he talked about the excitement of seeing his father's work on TV:

> *We had just moved from Tulsa [Oklahoma] to Little Rock [Arkansas], and I went in and that was the first thing I wanted to see was the moon landing, and we watched it.*

When asked how it made his father feel to see the success of his work, Bill added with a laugh:

> *How about over the moon?*

But Bill's father wasn't only excited about his own achievements, he was excited about the collective accomplishments of all the men and women who worked so hard to land a person on the moon. Bill said:

> *He was just so ecstatic ... It wasn't so much that he felt like, "Wow look what I did," it was like, "Look what we did."*

FAST FACT

THE MOON LANDING IS STILL ONE OF THE MOST HIGHLY WATCHED TELEVISION EVENTS IN U.S. HISTORY. ABOUT 125 MILLION VIEWERS TUNED IN TO SEE THE LANDING LIVE ON TV.

ARTISTS NEEDED

Even artists were needed to work in the Apollo Program. Safety manuals and diagrams of the spacecraft were important to the mission. Bill Ragan did some work in this area. Gesturing to show the thickness of the manuals he worked on, he said:

FAST FACT

NASA HAS ALSO WORKED WITH MANY ARTISTS THROUGH THEIR ARTIST'S COOPERATION PROGRAM, WHICH WAS ESTABLISHED IN 1962. IT WAS CREATED TO HAVE FINE ARTISTS CREATE WORK TO SHOW THE CULTURAL SIGNIFICANCE OF THE SPACE PROGRAM.

I did schematics, and I also did artist conceptions for the foldout manuals that they had. They could be this thick.

Bill continued, indicating how quickly the work had to be done. NASA employed artists like Bill, as well as technical writers and designers to create these schematics and manuals.

HOW YOU SEE HISTORY

1. What other kinds of jobs, not detailed in this chapter, do you think were essential to the success of the moon landing?
2. What do you think it was like for the astronauts to spend eight days together in the Command Module? How would you handle spending such a long time in such a small space?
3. Why do you think it is important for artists to document historic moments, such as the moon landing?

CHAPTER THREE

A ROCKET TO THE MOON

The moon landing marked an incredible accomplishment for the United States, as well as the attainment of the goal Kennedy had announced back in 1961. Not everyone believed the government would be able to follow through on that goal—and it certainly was not easy—but seeing the landing live on television made a lot of people realize what the U.S. space program was capable of. In an interview, Dr. Stanley Feld remembered the moment the landing happened:

> *I remember, I was at Parkland Memorial Hospital Residence Lounge when they landed on the moon, and that was exhilarating...[Kennedy] said that in 10 years we're going to land on the moon...the government did something...[it showed an] incredible* **dichotomy** *between what the government can do and what they can't do.*

It might be hard to imagine just how much work went into the historic event, but building a spacecraft that could safely bring two men to the moon and back, along with a third who stayed in orbit, was anything but simple. Each piece of equipment involved in

Scan this QR code to watch Dr. Stanley Feld tell his memories of the moon landing, as well as to hear Michael Collins discuss some of the technology used in the flight.

President Kennedy spoke about his intentions of reaching the moon at Rice University in 1962. He famously said that the United States could choose to go to the moon because it was hard and having that goal could measure their skills.

FAST FACT

DESPITE PREVIOUSLY STATING A DETERMINATION TO WIN THE SPACE RACE, KENNEDY ACTUALLY PROPOSED A JOINT MISSION TO THE MOON BETWEEN THE UNITED STATES AND SOVIET UNION DURING A UNITED NATIONS SPEECH IN 1963.

the journey required skill and understanding to both build and operate. Perhaps the most important aspect was the rocket that would help the spacecraft reach the moon.

REACHING NEW HEIGHTS

To land a man to the moon, the people of NASA knew they would need their most powerful rocket yet. That's where the Saturn V rocket came in. A type of rocket known as a heavy lift vehicle, the Saturn V needed to be the most powerful rocket to ever fly.

The Saturn V was developed and built in Huntsville, Alabama, at NASA's Marshall Space Flight Center. NASA had already built two smaller Saturn rockets, the Saturn I (1) and IB (1b). These rockets were used to launch spacecraft and people into orbit around Earth. The Saturn V was built to send people even further. It would bring astronauts beyond Earth orbit, all the way to the moon. The first Saturn V rocket launched in 1967 with Apollo 4. Another launched with Apollo 6 in 1968. These launches were to test the Saturn V rocket, but neither one had crews on board.

The Saturn V rocket was about the size of a 36-story building and 60 feet (80 meters) taller than the Statue of Liberty!

EARLIER SATURN ROCKETS

The mission to build a rocket like a Saturn rocket began in 1957, before NASA even existed. A group of engineers with the Army Ballistic Missile Agency were looking to build a rocket with the most powerful thrust yet. The next year, the Department of Defense formally authorized the project, and on February 3, 1959, it was given the name Saturn. The name was chosen because the rockets were considered an evolution of the previous Jupiter rockets. Being the next planet beyond Jupiter, the name Saturn made sense.

Initially called the *Saturn C-I* (later shortened to *Saturn I*), the first rocket built upon the technology and hardware used on earlier rockets like the Jupiter rockets. After a period of rigorous tests, the first Saturn rocket launched on October 27, 1961, from Cape Canaveral, Florida. The rocket continued with nine more successful launches, during which uncrewed test versions of Apollo spacecraft and satellites were placed into Earth orbit.

The upgraded version of the *Saturn I* was the *Saturn IB*. It was used for both crewed and uncrewed Apollo missions, which started in 1966. In October 1968, a *Saturn IB* launched the first crewed Apollo mission, *Apollo 7*, into orbit around Earth. *Saturn IB* rockets were also used to bring astronauts to the first U.S. space station, called Skylab, and for the U.S.-Soviet Apollo-Soyuz Test Project in 1975.

The first *Saturn I* rocket was about 180 feet (55 m) tall.

After the successful unmanned launches, Saturn V was ready to launch with a crew onboard. The first of these flights was *Apollo 8*, launched December 21, 1968. It was the first time a flight crew went beyond low Earth orbit and orbited the moon. *Apollo 9* and *Apollo 10* were also launched using Saturn V rockets.

FAST FACT

APOLLO 10 **WAS A TEST MISSION THAT HAS BEEN DESCRIBED AS THE "DRESS REHEARSAL" FOR THE MOON LANDING. IT TESTED ALL ASPECTS OF THE MISSION BESIDES THE ACTUAL LANDING.**

Apollo 7 **transmitted the first live television broadcast from an American-manned spacecraft. Walter Schirra, right, one of the Mercury 7, was the commander of the flight.**

Michael Collins stayed in the Command Module while Aldrin and Armstrong landed on the moon. He is seen here in the Command Module Simulator, about a month before *Apollo 11* launched.

By the time of *Apollo 11*, which launched on July 16, 1969, experts were confident a Saturn V could get the men to the moon. In an interview, Command Module Pilot Michael Collins talked about the intricacies of the Saturn V rocket:

> *This trip of ours to the moon may have looked to you simple or easy. I'd like to assure you that that has not been the case. The Saturn V rocket which put us into orbit is an incredibly complicated piece of machinery, every piece of which works flawlessly. This computer up above my head has a 38,000-word vocabulary, each word of which has been very carefully chosen to be of the utmost value to us, the crew.*

A ROCKET'S JOURNEY

During each of the *Saturn*-V-powered Apollo missions, the Saturn V had three stages. Each stage featured multiple engines that burned until their fuel was exhausted. After the first and second stages

Launch Complex 39 is still in use today. It was originally built for the Apollo program, but was later modified to be used for the space shuttle program.

NASA scientists used the effects of the Saturn V's third stage hitting the moon's surface to study moonquakes.

FAST FACT

EVERY SATURN V ROCKET FROM APOLLO MISSIONS TOOK OFF FROM LAUNCH COMPLEX 39 AT THE JOHN F. KENNEDY SPACE CENTER IN FLORIDA.

completed their burns, they would detach from the rocket and fall back to Earth, with the next stage taking over.

In the first stage, five F-1 engines lifted the rocket quickly enough to escape Earth's gravity. This stage took less than three minutes from takeoff. The second stage used five J-2 engines and lasted about six minutes, helping the spacecraft reach higher than 100 miles (160 km) in altitude.

The third stage was made up of just one J-2 engine that would burn two separate times. The first ignition would put the spacecraft into orbit. Then the engine would shut down, eventually reigniting a second time to bring the spacecraft to the moon. Rather than falling back to Earth, during all the Apollo missions, the third stage would either stay in space or fall to the moon's surface. During *Apollo 11*, after the third stage separated, it went into orbit around the sun.

HOW YOU SEE HISTORY

1. Why do you think it was important for the people of the United States to see Kennedy's goal of landing men on the moon occur within the time period he said it would?
2. Do you think the Saturn V rocket was the most important part of the spacecraft that helped man walk on the moon? Why or why not?
3. Besides studying moonquakes, how else do you think the release of the stages into space could be studied to help further space exploration?

CHAPTER FOUR

EVERYONE IS WATCHING

On the morning of July 20, 1969, Armstrong and Aldrin crawled through a tunnel from the Command Module into the Lunar Module. Collins stayed behind to operate the Command Module. Toward the end of the spacecraft's 12th orbit around the moon, the two modules separated. Armstrong and Aldrin began their trip from lunar orbit to the moon's surface in Lunar Module *Eagle*.

Five times during the descent, an alarm went off from the guidance computer, saying that the memory was full. Earlier **simulations** had shown that the landing could still occur if this happened, so Armstrong and Aldrin continued toward the moon's surface. About 500 feet (150 meters) above the surface, Armstrong started manually steering the spacecraft to avoid landing in a crater. A few minutes later, *Eagle* landed on the moon. The landing area was known as the Sea of **Tranquility**. It was chosen for landing because of its smooth and level **terrain**.

At 4:17 p.m. EDT, Armstrong radioed down to Earth, saying, "Houston, Tranquility Base here. The *Eagle* has landed."

Scan this QR code to watch Robert Applebaum and others talk about the moon landing.

The crew cabin of the Lunar Module was also known as the ascent stage.

LUNAR TOUCHDOWN

Another famous quote that came from the moon landing—perhaps the most famous one—was Neil Armstrong's, "That's one small step for man, one giant leap for mankind." Those were the words he said on July 20, 1969, at 10:56 p.m. EDT, as he stepped out of the module and onto the moon's surface. About 20 minutes later, Aldrin joined Armstrong on the surface of the moon.

Armstrong observed that the surface of the moon was "fine and powdery."

WHO IS HOUSTON?

You often hear astronauts talking to "Houston." Maybe you have even said the famous phrase, "Houston, we have a problem," when something has gone wrong. But who is "Houston" anyway?

As you might have guessed, Houston is not one person, but a reference to the city of Houston, Texas, where you can find the Lyndon B. Johnson Space Center. This is the space center where NASA's Mission Control Center is located. When radioing down to the control center, astronauts use the **call sign** *Houston*.

The Mission Control Center is staffed by a large ground control team. They monitor, support, and advise astronauts in space. It is always crucial for astronauts in space to maintain constant communication with the Mission Control Center. It was especially important during the first moon landing, since they were doing something that had never been done before.

Even when there is not an active mission to the moon, the control center is staffed 24 hours a day, 7 days a week. Today, the flight controllers who work out of Houston monitor the International Space Station and the astronauts on board at all times of day. They also help prepare for future space missions. They plan out spacewalks and other activities astronauts need to do while in space. They also set up simulations to help prepare for all possible outcomes that could happen during a flight. No matter what the problem in space may be, Houston, or mission control, is always there to answer the call.

This is what Mission Control Center looked like at the end of *Apollo 11*.

FAST FACT

ARMSTRONG HAD PREPARED TO SAY, "THAT'S ONE SMALL STEP FOR A MAN, ONE GIANT LEAP FOR MANKIND." BUT IN THE EXCITEMENT, HE FORGOT TO SAY "A."

Armstrong and Aldrin spent more than two hours walking on the moon. They set up a tool to measure the composition of solar winds that reached the moon. They also set up a device that could receive laser beams from observato-

Aldrin sets up a tool to monitor seismic activity on the moon.

"All the News That's Fit to Print"

The New York Times

LATE CITY EDITION

Weather: Rain, warm today; clear tonight. Sunny, pleasant tomorrow. Temp. range: today 80-66; Sunday 71-66. Temp.-Hum. Index yesterday 69. Complete U.S. report on P., 50.

VOL. CXVIII. No. 40,721 — NEW YORK, MONDAY, JULY 21, 1969 — 10 CENTS

MEN WALK ON MOON

ASTRONAUTS LAND ON PLAIN; COLLECT ROCKS, PLANT FLAG

Voice From Moon: 'Eagle Has Landed'

EAGLE (the lunar module): Houston, Tranquility Base here. The Eagle has landed.

HOUSTON: Roger, Tranquility, we copy you on the ground. You've got a bunch of guys about to turn blue. We're breathing again. Thanks a lot.

TRANQUILITY BASE: Thank you.

HOUSTON: You're looking good here.

TRANQUILITY BASE: A very smooth touchdown.

HOUSTON: Eagle, you are stay for T1. [The first step in the lunar operation.] Over.

TRANQUILITY BASE: Roger. Stay for T1.

HOUSTON: Roger and we see you venting the ox.

TRANQUILITY BASE: Roger.

COLUMBIA (the command and service module): How do you read me?

HOUSTON: Columbia, he has landed Tranquility Base. Eagle is at Tranquility. I read you five by. Over.

COLUMBIA: Yes, I heard the whole thing.

HOUSTON: Well, it's a good show.

COLUMBIA: Fantastic.

TRANQUILITY BASE: I'll second that.

APOLLO CONTROL: The next major stay-no stay will be for the T2 event. That is at 21 minutes 26 seconds after initiation of power descent.

COLUMBIA: Up telemetry command reset to reacquire on high gain.

HOUSTON: Copy. Out.

APOLLO CONTROL: We have an unofficial time for that touchdown of 102 hours, 45 minutes, 42 seconds and we will update that.

HOUSTON: Eagle, you loaded R2 wrong. We want 10254.

TRANQUILITY BASE: Roger. Do you want the horizontal 55 15.2?

HOUSTON: That's affirmative.

APOLLO CONTROL: We're now less than four minutes from our next stay-no stay. It will be for one complete revolution of the command module.

One of the first things that Armstrong and Aldrin will do after getting their next stay-no stay will be to remove their helmets and gloves.

HOUSTON: Eagle, you are stay for T2. Over.

Continued on Page 4, Col. 1

VOYAGE TO THE MOON

By Archibald MacLeish

PRESENCE among us,

wanderer in our skies,

dazzle of silver in our leaves and on our
waters silver,

O
silver evasion in our farthest thought—
"the visiting moon" . . . "the glimpses of the moon" . . .

and we have touched you!

From the first of time,
before the first of time, before the
first men tasted time, we thought of you.
You were a wonder to us, unattainable,
a longing past the reach of longing,
a light beyond our light, our lives—perhaps
a meaning to us . . .

Now
our hands have touched you in your depth of night.

Three days and three nights we journeyed,
steered by farthest stars, climbed outward,
crossed the invisible tide-rip where the floating dust
falls one way or the other in the void between,
followed that other down, encountered
cold, faced death—unfathomable emptiness . . .

Then, the fourth day evening, we descended,
made fast, set foot at dawn upon your beaches,
sifted between our fingers your cold sand.

We stand here in the dusk, the cold, the silence . . .

and here, as at the first of time, we lift our heads.
Over us, more beautiful than the moon, a
moon, a wonder to us, unattainable,
a longing past the reach of longing,
a light beyond our light, our lives—perhaps
a meaning to us . . .

O, a meaning!

over us on these silent beaches the bright
earth,
presence among us

Neil A. Armstrong moves away from the leg of the landing craft after taking the first step on the surface of the moon

The New York Times from C.B.S. News

Col. Edwin E. Aldrin Jr. climbing down the ladder. The television camera was attached to a side of the lunar module.

Associated Press

Mr. Armstrong, right, and Colonel Aldrin raise the U.S. flag. A metal rod at right angles to the mast keeps flag unfurled.

A Powdery Surface Is Closely Explored

By JOHN NOBLE WILFORD
Special to The New York Times

HOUSTON, Monday, July 21—Men have landed and walked on the moon.

Two Americans, astronauts of Apollo 11, steered their fragile four-legged lunar module safely and smoothly to the historic landing yesterday at 4:17:40 P.M., Eastern daylight time.

Neil A. Armstrong, the 38-year-old civilian commander, radioed to earth and the mission control room here:

"Houston, Tranquility Base here. The Eagle has landed."

The first men to reach the moon—Mr. Armstrong and his co-pilot, Col. Edwin E. Aldrin Jr. of the Air Force—brought their ship to rest on a level, rock-strewn plain near the southwestern shore of the arid Sea of Tranquility.

About six and a half hours later, Mr. Armstrong opened the landing craft's hatch, stepped slowly down the ladder and declared as he planted the first human footprint on the lunar crust:

"That's one small step for man, one giant leap for mankind."

His first step on the moon came at 10:56:20 P.M., as a television camera outside the craft transmitted his every move to an awed and excited audience of hundreds of millions of people on earth.

Tentative Steps Test Soil

Mr. Armstrong's initial steps were tentative tests of the lunar soil's firmness and of his ability to move about easily in his bulky white spacesuit and backpacks and under the influence of lunar gravity, which is one-sixth that of the earth.

"The surface is fine and powdery," the astronaut reported. "I can pick it up loosely with my toe. It does adhere in fine layers like powdered charcoal to the sole and sides of my boots. I only go in a small fraction of an inch, maybe an eighth of an inch. But I can see the footprints of my boots in the treads in the fine sandy particles.

After 15 minutes of Mr. Armstrong's testing, Colonel Aldrin joined him outside the craft.

The two men got busy setting up another television camera out from the lunar module, planting an American flag into the ground, scooping up soil and rock samples, deploying scientific experiments and hopping and loping about in a demonstration of their lunar agility.

They found walking and working on the moon less taxing than had been forecast. Mr. Armstrong once reported he was "very comfortable."

And people back on earth found the black-and-white television pictures of the bug-shaped lunar module and the men tramping about it so sharp and clear as to seem unreal, more like a toy and toy-like figures than human beings on the most daring and far-reaching expedition thus far undertaken.

Nixon Telephones Congratulations

During one break in the astronauts' work, President Nixon congratulated them from the White House in what, he said, "certainly has to be the most historic telephone call ever made."

"Because of what you have done," the President told the astronauts, "the heavens have become a part of man's world. And as you talk to us from the Sea of Tranquility it requires us to redouble our efforts to bring peace and tranquility to earth.

"For one priceless moment in the whole history of man all the people on this earth are truly one—one in their pride in what you have done and one in our prayers that you will return safely to earth."

Mr. Armstrong replied:

"Thank you Mr. President. It's a great honor and privilege for us to be here representing not only the United States but men of peace of all nations, men with interests and a curiosity and men with a vision for the future."

Mr. Armstrong and Colonel Aldrin returned to their landing craft and closed the hatch at 1:12 A.M., 2 hours 21 minutes after opening the hatch on the moon. While the third member of the crew, Lieut. Col. Michael Collins of the Air Force, kept his orbital vigil overhead in the command ship, the two moon explorers settled down to sleep.

Outside their vehicle the astronauts had found a bleak

Continued on Page 2, Col. 1

Today's 4-Part Issue of The Times

This morning's issue of The New York Times is divided into four parts. The first part is devoted to news of Apollo 11, and includes Editorials and letters to the Editor (Page 16). Poems on the landing on the moon appear on Page 17.

General news begins on the first page of the second part. The News Summary and Index is on the first page of the third part, which includes sports news, obituaries (Page 51) and transportation news and weather reports (Pages 50 and 52).

Financial and business news begins on the first page of the fourth part.

Following is the News Index for today's issue:

The front page of the *New York Times* covers the moon landing in an edition for July 21, 1969.

ries on Earth and measure the exact distance between the two places. They also set up a **seismometer** to measure moonquakes and impacts from meteors. They took many photographs and brought back rock and soil samples to be studied back on Earth. The machines they set up and the items they brought back would continue to be used long after the men left the moon.

FAST FACT

TODAY, THE PHRASE "THE EAGLE HAS LANDED" IS OFTEN USED TO MEAN SOMEONE OR SOMETHING HAS ARRIVED OR AN IMPORTANT TASK HAS BEEN COMPLETED. THIS EXPRESSION COMES FROM ARMSTRONG'S USE OF IT DURING THE MOON LANDING.

SOMETHING TO REMEMBER

Back on Earth, everyone was watching the historic moment. It was broadcast on television worldwide, talked about on the radio, and reported in newspapers. People were excited to be able to see the accomplishment with their own eyes. Robert Applebaum detailed his memories from that day:

> *I remember I was at home watching it in our living room on, I believe, a black-and-white TV if you can still remember that. It is something that I will remember…to hear those words, it's one of those things you'll never forget.*

Many people shared Robert's sentiment of the landing being a moment they'd never forget. And there was no shortage of things people could buy to help them remember. Commemorative coins were one popular way to remember. In fact, a coin known as the Eisenhower dollar coin, or silver dollar, featured the *Apollo 11* **insignia** on one side.

Another popular keepsake to celebrate the moon landing was a collectible postage stamp. At just 10 cents, it was an affordable way to remember the historic moment. In an interview, a woman remembered buying them for her children:

> *I even ordered my kids the stamps that you could get at that time and had it mailed to us so that they'd all have a moon landing stamp. So that was exciting.*

Michael Collins designed the *Apollo 11* insignia, used for patches on the astronauts' suits, and later on the back of the Eisenhower dollar.

President Richard Nixon gave all 50 U.S. states and each of its territories moon rock samples to display in 1970.

A stamp for the moon landing was released on September 9, 1969. The astronauts had brought the master die that would be used to make the stamps with them to the moon.

HOW YOU SEE HISTORY

1. Why do you think "The eagle has landed" caught on as a popular catchphrase?
2. Why do you think it was important for the astronauts to stay in constant communication with ground control?
3. What do you think scientists were able to learn from the tools set up by Armstrong and Aldrin on the moon?

FAST FACT

AT THE TIME IT WAS RELEASED, THE MOON LANDING STAMP WAS THE LARGEST STAMP THE UNITED STATES HAD EVER CREATED.

CHAPTER FIVE

ALL EYES ON THE SKY

A unique thing about the moon is that you can see it from anywhere on Earth. So it wasn't just in the United States that people were waiting for and watching the moon landing. People were watching all around the world. Americans living abroad, Soviets keeping up with the Space Race, and anyone else in a place where news could be broadcast was paying attention. In an interview, David Watson and Colonel Bob Bullock shared what it was like to be in other countries during the moon landing.

ONE MOON

No matter where you are on Earth, if you look up at the moon, you are seeing the same **celestial** body someone else might be looking at from the other side of the world. In an interview, David recalled being abroad when the moon landing occurred:

I remember, I was on the river when they were on the moon, and over in Vietnam you got a lot of full moons. And I remember my enginemen and I, we were on the river and we looked up [and thought] "there's somebody on that moon." I think that was a pretty significant

Scan this QR code to watch David Watson and Colonel Bob Bullock tell their story of being in other countries during the moon landing.

Millions of people around the world watched the moon landing on TV, even the pope! This photo shows Pope Paul VI watching the event from the Vatican Observatory in Italy.

> *event. It really was. That's an accomplishment by our country.*

Colonel Bullock was also outside of the United States when the moon landing happened. He was in Germany and remembers being up in the middle of the night with his family watching the historic moment on television:

> *We were in Germany during the moon landing, and we were able to actually see it live on Armed Forces Television because they could patch into NASA's videos…it happened over there at some unholy time, 2 or 3 o'clock in the morning…but [we] were just sitting there awestruck.*

FAST FACT

AS ARMSTRONG CLIMBED OUT OF THE LUNAR MODULE, HE PULLED A LEVER TO RELEASE A CAMERA FROM THE SPACECRAFT. IT SENT A BROADCAST DOWN TO EARTH. ARMSTRONG LATER REMOVED THE CAMERA AND SET IT UP ON A TRIPOD. THE CAMERA WAS LEFT ON THE MOON WHEN THE MEN RETURNED TO EARTH.

LEAVING THEIR MARK

Besides the scientific equipment left behind to continue studying the moon's environment after they left, Aldrin and Armstrong left a few other things behind on the moon. Perhaps most famously, they planted an American flag on the lunar surface.

Other items left behind on the moon were mostly abandoned to limit the amount of material brought back into the spacecraft. To make it back to the Command Module safely, it was important to keep the Lunar Module as light as possible. Considering they were bringing back heavy samples of rock, this meant leaving behind whatever they could. Both astronauts (as well as many future astronauts who went to the moon) left their lunar overshoes, the bulky footwear that protected their feet during the moonwalk, behind on the moon. They also tossed unneeded tools, cameras, and even bags of human waste from the Lunar Module.

Other items left behind included symbolic tributes, such as a tiny disk etched with messages of goodwill from Presidents Eisenhower, Kennedy, Johnson, and Nixon. They also left a plaque saying that people from

Aldrin and Armstrong were the first, but not the last, to leave an American flag on the moon. Astronauts from each Apollo mission that landed on the moon left a flag.

COMING HOME

After nearly a full day on the moon, Armstrong and Aldrin returned to *Eagle*. The module launched and returned to lunar orbit before reconnecting with *Columbia*. The astronauts climbed

Earth were the first to walk on the moon and that they came in peace. The plaque also includes the date of the landing. There was also an *Apollo 1* patch to honor the three astronauts who died in the 1967 fire. They didn't only honor Americans though; Armstrong and Aldrin also left medals to honor late Russian cosmonauts Yuri Gagarin and Vladimir Komarov.

With no wind or flowing water on the moon, the footprints Aldrin and Armstrong left on the moon still appear to be intact today.

back into the Command Module to join Collins. About four hours later, the Lunar Module detached from the Command Module, remaining in orbit as the astronauts made their way back home inside the Command Module.

A group of people in Hamburg, Germany, gather on a sidewalk outside a display window to watch the launch of *Apollo 11*.

FAST FACT

NO ONE KNOWS FOR SURE WHERE EAGLE IS NOW. IT IS LIKELY EITHER STILL ORBITING THE MOON OR IT MAY HAVE EXPLODED DUE TO LEAKING FUEL OR AGING BATTERIES.

On July 22, at around noon EDT, the Command Module left lunar orbit and headed back toward Earth. About 44 hours later, on July 24, re-entry procedures began. *Apollo 11* was nearly ready to land, but it wouldn't be coming down on solid ground—it would be splashing down into the Pacific Ocean! A parachute was deployed to help the spacecraft safely enter the water. The exact landing point changed by about 250 miles (400 km) from the intended location because of bad weather, but the recovery ship, *USS Hornet*, was waiting just 13 miles (20 km) away to pick up the crew.

Upon returning to Earth, the crew had to immediately enter quarantine. This was done in case the moon had any biological **pathogens** that the astronauts carried with them. They entered the mobile quarantine facility (MQF) aboard the *Hornet*. The

Aldrin and Armstrong both climbed down a ladder to get from the Lunar Module to the moon's surface.

The Command Module splashed down at 12:51 EDT on July 24, 1969. It was about 900 miles (1,450 km) from the coast of Hawai'i.

FAST FACT

FROM THE TIME THE LUNAR MODULE LEFT THE MOON TO THE TIME THE COMMAND MODULE SPLASHED DOWN WAS ABOUT 71 HOURS—JUST SHY OF THREE FULL DAYS. THE ENTIRE JOURNEY WAS A LITTLE MORE THAN 195 HOURS, OR MORE THAN 8 DAYS.

MQF was a converted Airstream trailer that had an area for sleeping, a kitchen, and a bathroom. They were transported inside the MQF from the *Hornet* to the Pearl Harbor Naval Base in Hawai'i. They were then taken to another base in Hawai'i where the MQF was loaded into a plane to be flown to the Ellington Air Force Base in Houston,

Upon the return of *Apollo 11*, President Nixon greeted the astronauts from outside a window of the MQF.

FAST FACT

THE ASTRONAUTS STILL HAD TO WORK WHILE IN QUARANTINE. THEY COMPLETED REPORTS AND GAVE BRIEFINGS TO THE *APOLLO 12* CREW, WHO WOULD TAKE FLIGHT JUST A FEW MONTHS LATER. THEY DID, HOWEVER, TAKE TIME TO CELEBRATE ARMSTRONG'S 39TH BIRTHDAY WHILE IN QUARANTINE.

Texas. There, the men were able to enter a somewhat more spacious quarantine facility. In all, they had to remain in quarantine for 21 days from the time they were first exposed to lunar material.

INTERNATIONAL CELEBRITIES

On August 10, 1969, when the three astronauts officially left quarantine, they were already world famous. They spent a day reuniting with their families before it was right back to work. They held a press conference on August 12. The next day they traveled to New York and Chicago for parades, before ending the night in Los Angeles for a state dinner hosted by the president. They returned to Houston for another parade on August 16.

People in Paris, France, gather to watch the astronauts drive past in their motorcade.

On September 29, 1969, the three astronauts and their wives began the Giantstep Goodwill World Tour, at the request of President Nixon. Over seven weeks, they traveled to six continents. They met with presidents, prime ministers, kings, queens, and ambassadors. The astronauts were given numerous awards and held 22 press conferences. It was estimated that more than 100 million people around the world saw them in various conferences and motorcades. It was clear their "giant leap" had made an impact all over the world.

HOW YOU SEE HISTORY

1. Why do you think it was such a big deal for people—even outside of the United States—to watch the moon landing on television?
2. If you met the astronauts on their world tour and had the opportunity to ask them one question, what would it be?
3. Would you travel to the moon if given the chance? Why or why not?

TIMELINE

PREVIOUS PIONEERS: TIMELINE OF THE MOON LANDING

1958: NASA is created.

1959: The first seven astronauts are chosen for Project Mercury. They become known as the Mercury 7.

May 5, 1961: Alan Shepard becomes the first American in space.

February 20, 1962: John Glenn becomes the first American to orbit Earth.

January 27, 1967: A fire breaks out during a preflight test of *Apollo 1*, killing astronauts Virgil Grissom, Edward White, and Roger Chaffee.

1966: The first uncrewed Apollo missions begin.

A TEAM EFFORT: TIMELINE OF THE MOON LANDING

May 25, 1961: President John F. Kennedy announces the goal to safely land a man on the moon before the end of the decade.

A ROCKET TO THE MOON: TIMELINE OF THE MOON LANDING

October 1968: *Apollo 7*, the first crewed Apollo mission, orbits Earth.

July 16, 1969: *Apollo 11* launches from Cape Kennedy.

EVERYONE IS WATCHING: TIMELINE OF THE MOON LANDING

July 20, 1969: *Eagle* lands on the moon. Armstrong becomes the first man to walk on the moon. Aldrin becomes the second about 20 minutes later.

July 21, 1969: *Eagle* leaves the moon and docks with *Columbia*. Aldrin and Armstrong return to the Command Module with Collins.

ALL EYES ON THE SKY: TIMELINE OF THE MOON LANDING

July 22, 1969: Command Module *Columbia* leaves lunar orbit.

July 24, 1969: Command Module *Columbia* splashes down into the Pacific Ocean with Aldrin, Armstrong, and Collins.

August 10, 1969: *Aldrin, Armstrong, and Collins leave quarantine.*

GLOSSARY

aeronautics: The science of flight.

Apollo-Soyuz Test Project: The first crewed international space mission, conducted jointly by the United States and the Soviet Union in July 1975.

call sign: The combination of identifying letters, numbers, or words assigned to an operator, office, activity, vehicle, or station for use in communication.

celestial: Of or relating to the sky.

civilian: A person not on active duty in the military.

cosmonaut: An astronaut of the Soviet or Russian space program.

depressurization: The act of pressure being released from a spacecraft.

dichotomy: A division or difference between two opposite things.

die: A device used for cutting, stamping, or shaping an object.

insignia: A distinguishing mark or emblem.

nuclear: Science related to the nuclei of atoms.

pathogen: Something that causes a disease.

schematic: A drawing or diagram showing the main parts or workings of something.

seismometer: A tool that measures the movements of the ground.

simulation: A representation of the operation of a process by means of another system.

Space Race: A period of competition between the Soviet Union and the United States over who could conquer space exploration first.

suborbital: Involving less than one orbit.

supersonic: Faster than the speed of sound.

technician: A person whose job involves the practical use of machines or science.

terrain: A type of land in an area.

thruster: An engine that develops force by expelling a jet of fluid or a stream of particles.

tranquility: The state of being calm and free from disturbance.

transmission: A message or broadcast sent via electrical signals to a radio, television, or computer.

FOR MORE INFORMATION

BOOKS

Clark, Stuart. *Space*. Buffalo, NY: Cavendish Square Publishing, 2025.

Gifford, Clive. *Out of This World Space Tech*. Buffalo, NY: Cavendish Square Publishing, 2024.

Idzikowski, Lisa. *One Giant Leap: America's Mission to the Moon*. Minneapolis, MN: Lerner Publications, 2026.

Krensky, Stephen. *Moon Landing: The Incredible Story of the Apollo 11 Mission*. New York, NY: DK Children, 2026.

Reynolds, Donna. *Humans in Space*. Buffalo, NY: Cavendish Square Publishing, 2024.

WEBSITES

Apollo 11

airandspace.si.edu/explore/stories/apollo-11-moon-landing

Learn all about the moon landing, from Kennedy's early speeches to the astronauts and spacecraft that made it happen.

Apollo 11 Artifacts

www.si.edu/spotlight/apollo-11

View photos and read about artifacts from Apollo 11 held at the Smithsonian's National Air and Space Museum.

The Apollo Program

www.nasa.gov/the-apollo-program/

Learn all about the Apollo Program on NASA's official website.

The Moon Landing

kids.nationalgeographic.com/history/article/moon-landing

Read about the Space Race and watch a short video on the first moon walk.

Who Was John Glenn?

www.nasa.gov/learning-resources/for-kids-and-students/who-was-john-glenn-grades-5-8/

Find more facts about John Glenn in this article from NASA.

INDEX

G

H

I

J

K

L

M

N

O

P

Q

R

S

T

U

W

PHOTO CREDITS

Cover, pp. 7, 9, 13, 15, 17, 20, 21, 29, 30, 31, 32, 37, 39, 49, 51, 52, 53 courtesy of NASA; p. 10 agsaz/Shutterstock.com; p. 11 NASA/Life Magazine; p. 16 NASA/Bob Nye; p. 22 Apollo Spacecraft diagram/ Wikimedia Commons; p. 23 NASM-NASM2013-0266/Wikimedia Commons; p. 24 Bill Waterson/Alamy Photos; p. 28 JFK at Rice University/Wikimedia Commons; p. 33 Space Shuttle Atlantis at Launch Pad 39A/Wikimedia Commons; p. 34 AS07-3-1545/ Wikimedia Commons; p. 38 J Marshall - Tribaleye Images/Alamy Photos; p. 40 PA Images/Alamy Photos; p. 41 Futuras Fotos/Alamy Photos; p. 43 (top) Apollo 11 insignia/Wikimedia Commons; p. 43 (bottom) 1974S Eisenhower Reverse/Wikimedia Commons; p. 44 Mark Scheuern/Alamy Photos; p. 45 First Man on Moon 1969 Issue-10c/Wikimedia Commons; p. 47 RealyEasyStar/ FotograKa Felici/ Alamy Photos; p. 48 Universal Images Group North America LLC/ Alamy Photos; p. 50 INTERFOTO/Alamy Photos; p. 54 Keystone Press/Alamy Photos.

ABOUT THE AUTHOR

KATE MIKOLEY has written dozens of nonfiction books for children and teens. She has a bachelor's degree in journalism and a love for fact-checking that can sometimes be misconstrued as a passion for proving people wrong.

When she's not writing, Kate can often be found crocheting, reading, attempting to learn a new craft, or swimming. While she enjoys traveling, she currently has no plans to visit the moon; she does, however, enjoy looking up at it when she takes her beloved dog, Otty, out for his nightly strolls.